THE BASICS OF MAKING HOMEMADE CHEESE

HOW TO MAKE AND STORE HARD AND SOFT CHEESES, YOGURT, TOFU, CHEESE CULTURES, AND VEGETABLE RENNET

DAVID NASH

PREFACE

Since you are reading a book on self-reliance, I am assuming you want to know more about how to take care of yourself in disaster situations

I would like to suggest you take a moment and visit my website and YouTube channel for thousands of hours of free content related to basic preparedness concepts

Dave's Homestead Website
https://www.tngun.com

Dave's Homestead YouTube Channel
https://www.youtube.com/tngun

Shepherd Publishing
https://www.shepherdpublish.com

$$1$$

WHY MAKE CHEESE?

When I started my path to learning how to be more self reliant Cheese-making and Soap-making appeared to be magical skills far beyond my meager abilities. Frankly I was a little scared to try them. Then, while cruising around the local home-brew/organic gardening store, I found a how to make mozzarella kit. I splurged and made my first homemade cheese.

It was wonderful. It was easy, and it was something that my wife was impressed by (of course I hid the kit)…

Seriously through, I found cheesemaking to be a great hobby. It is a rare skill that is alway a hit as a gift or something to take to a party. Like my other forays into DIY, this simple mozzarella kit grew out of control.

In this book I will show how to make farmhouse cheddar cheese, Yogurts, cream cheese, Ghee, Tofu, Seitan, DIY equipment, Rennet, and Cheese Cultures.

There are all manner of websites and classes for home cheese making as this is a great hobby, especially if you are a homesteader with a goat or a cow. However, few classes include bean based non-dairy like Tofu, Cultures, and DIY equipment in a basic class.

Don't think home cheesemaking is too hard or too expensive, It's much easier than you think. With some very simple ingredients and equipment (That I will show you how to make) you could be putting fresh, homemade cheese on your dinner table tonight.

Think of the joy of giving a homemade gift basket full of homemade cheeses, wine, and soaps all hand made by you with love, using instructions from this Homestead Basics Series.

2

HOW TO MAKE FRESH MOZZARELLA CHEESE AT HOME

My very first foray into cheese making was using a Ricki Carroll kit "30 minute mozzarella". It turned out so good the first time, my wife immediately told me to get the hard cheese kit (I've gone a little overboard, and she may regret that a little since the fridge is full of "experiments" that haven't aged enough to try yet).

If you want to try cheesemaking at home, I highly recommend Ricki's book Home Cheese Making: Recipes for 75 Delicious Cheeses. I own it and think the recipes are well thought out to be as simple as possible.

Homemade Mozzarella is an extremely simple cheese to make, yet it tastes wonderful and is a great introduction to home cheese-making. Before I tried making my own mozzarella I thought cheese-making was only for highly skilled artisans and was beyond the reach of "normal" folks.

This is a simple recipe, and pretty easy to make as long as you follow the recipe step by step. (my only disaster was when I was trying to tape the procedure and spent to much time talking and not enough doing....)

30 Minute Mozzarella

Equipment

- 1 gallon pot, Stainless steel or enameled
- Thermometer
- Colander
- Slotted Spoon
- Long Knife
- Microwavable bowl

Ingredients

- 1 gallon milk
- 1 ½ teaspoon citric acid dissolved in 1 cup chlorine free water
- ¼ tablet (or 1/4 tsp of liquid) rennet dissolved in ¼ cup chlorine free water
- 1 tablespoon of cheese salt and/or herbs (optional – but I found it bland without salt)

Directions

1. Pour milk into pot and vigorously stir ion citric acid
2. Heat to 90^0F while stirring
3. Remove from heat and stir in the rennet solution with a dashing motion (up and down like making butter in an old fashioned dasher) for about 30 seconds
4. Cover pot and let sit for 5 minutes
5. If the curd looks like a white jello with a clear separation of the curd and the whey cut the curd into 1/2 "blocks (see Farmhouse cheddar video II)
6. Heat the curds to 105^0F while gently stirring curds
7. Take off burner and stir for another 2-5 minutes (longer time = firmer finished cheese)
8. Pour off floating whey (save it for bread making)

9. Ladle curds into large microwavable bowl and drain as much whey ass possible without pressing curds too hard. (You can press down a little, but don't mash it flat)
10. Microwave bowl for one minute
11. Ricki's kit also has a recipe for using hot water – but this is easier for me
12. Remove and drain as you gently fold curds into a single piece. (add salt now if desired)
13. Microwave for another 30 seconds. Drain and stretch.
14. cheese must be 135^0F to stretch – if its not hot enough microwave for another 30 seconds.
15. I used latex gloves to help with heat, as well as having a ice bath nearby to dip my hands in occasionally.
16. Dad told me I could grow up smart or strong – guess which one I picked.....LOL
17. Keep stretching cheese like taffy – the more you heat and stretch the firmer it will be.
18. When finished stretching submerge it in ice water to set the cheese.
19. Critical for texture and to prevent it from being grainy.)

Homemade mozzarella is the best when eaten warm right after it's made. Chilling the mozzarella will change its texture a bit, but I love it wight out of the original ice bath!

You can cube it up for skewers, slice it up for topping pizza or grilled cheese sandwiches, or partially freeze it, then shred it.

If you have extra, can even freeze the cheese successfully. In fact, some say that it melts better after it has been frozen and thawed!

HOW TO MAKE FARMHOUSE CHEDDAR CHEESE

Cheese making came into being as a way to preserve milk without refrigeration, and was a valuable part of historical life.

Making cheese in the modern age is more about enjoyment than survival, but it does help build planning skills and patience, both of which are essential to emergency planning.

Making cheese is not hard, but it does take a long time for your finished and waxed cheese to age properly (6-8 months).

For the cheese making purists, this is actually called farmhouse cheddar. This is a recipe that does not need the additional step of "cheddaring"

"Cheddaring" refers to an additional step in the production of Cheddar cheese where, after heating, the curd is kneaded with salt, cut into cubes to drain the whey, and then stacked and turned

To make cheese you will need a cheese press, and while you can certainly buy one. In a later chapter I will show you a way to make a simple press that works well and does not cost a lot of money.

How to Make Cheddar Cheese

Equipment

- Cheesecloth
- Colander
- Thermometer
- Cheese press
- String
- Slotted Spoon
- Large pot (stainless steel or unbroken enamel ONLY. Aluminum or cast iron will produce an off taste)
- Large bowl
- Measuring cups and spoons
- Wooden cutting board
- Timer

Ingredients

- 2 gallons milk
- 1 packet Mesophilic direct set culture
- ½ rennet tablet dissolved in ¼ cup chlorine free water
- 1 tablespoon cheese salt (or non-iodized salt)

Directions for Making Farmhouse Cheddar

1. Heat milk to 90°F (Goat milk to 85°F)
2. Add culture; stir well, let sit for 45 minutes while maintaining temperature
3. Add rennet by pouring gently through perforated spoon.
4. Stir very gently to bottom of bowl for at least 1 minute.
5. You may also "top stir" for, 1 minute, the first ½ inch to prevent cream separation if using goats milk.
6. Cover and let sit undisturbed for 45 minutes (until strong curd is formed).

7. Cut the curd into ½" blocks
8. Warm VERY gently to 100°F while stirring blocks gently. (Do this by placing pot into a sink of hot water and don't let the temperature of the pot rise more than 2°F every 5 minutes.
9. As the curd heats, and is stirred, the curds will separate from the whey and the curds will shrink.
10. Remove from heat, cover, and let curds settle for 5 minutes
11. Strain the curds into a cheesecloth lined colander (save the whey for Ricotta and for baking. Waste not …)
12. Knot one corner of the cheese cloth around the other three to form a bag.
13. Hang bag over pot for at least an hour.
14. Once the curds have drained, put them into a large bowl and mix with salt as you break curds into walnut sized pieces.

Directions for Molding the Farmhouse Cheddar

1. Firmly pack cheese into a cheesecloth lined mold, fold cheesecloth over top of curds.
2. Any wrinkles in the cheesecloth will translate into divots and marks in your finished cheese.
3. Apply 10 pounds of pressure to mold for 15 minutes (whey will drain from mold).
4. Flip mold and apply 20 pounds of pressure to other side of cheese for 12 hours.
5. Turn cheese again and apply 20 pounds for an additional 12 hours.
6. Remove cheese from mold, and carefully peel cloth away, taking care not to rip cheese.
7. Air dry the cheese at room temperature on a wooden board until a rind has developed (3 to 5 days). You must flip the cheese several times a day as moisture will collect on board if you don't.
8. Wax the cheese (or vacuum seal it) and age for at least 2

months. However, the longer it ages, the sharper it will be. (6-8 months).

4

HOW TO MAKE A MESOPHYLLIC CHEESE CULTURE

Cream cheese, sour cream, and a whole variety of cheeses use Mesophilic cultures to turn milk to cheese. Mose home cheesemakers use commercially purchased packages of powdered culture.

However, I wanted to know how it was done before we had big brown trucks to deliver the cultures.

I have been researching and found how extremely simple Mesophilic Cheese Starter is to make at home, I have used this in the recipes I am sharing, and it works. However, homemade cultures and rennets are a little more "touchy" than processed cultures, you may have to tweak the recipe from time to time.

This recipe uses a freezer, but I heard of an anecdotal story of how some eastern Europeans snuck their favorite yogurt cultures into the country through Ellis Island. It seems like the federal workers would open the jars of starter culture that our ancestors tried to import with them, smelled the yeastiness and threw the jars out.

After this became known to those planning to immigrate, one particularly resourceful lady dipped several of her lace heirlooms in the culture and let it dry. The inspectors did not notice the bacteria dried on the cloth and when she settled in her new country, she simply dipped the lace in some warm milk and let the bacteria inoculate it.

The Process is Simple:

All you need is a measuring cup, and ice cube tray, and some cultured buttermilk.

You see cultured buttermilk contains a small amount of Mesophilic bacteria, just not enough to really get a cheese going, but if you set about 2 cups worth out in a warm room for 8-10 hours the bacteria takes off and soon thickens the buttermilk and gives it a distinctive yeast smell.

If you take this thick buttermilk and pour it into a clean ice tray and freeze it each cube is the equivalent of once ounce of Mesophilic culture.

When you are ready to make cheese, simply drop one of these cubes in your milk and let it grow and multiply.

Just make sure to keep a couple of ice cubes back so you can use it to make more culture later. Once you get low you can just dump once of your culture cubes in some milk and let it sit until it is thick.

HOMEMADE CHEESE PRESS

A commercial cheese press can cost hundreds of dollars, while the one we are making today is only a fraction of the cost. It was this press that allowed me to try to make my own homemade hard cheeses, as my budget did not allow me to purchase a commercial press, even an inexpensive store bought press is $150.00 or more.

This press costs around $20 if you buy everything new, less than $10 if you can scrounge.

I imagine a creative person could even make their own molds from various PVC pipes if they desired.

Parts:

- Two hardwood boards, approximately 18 inches long, ½ to ¾ inch thick, and 6-8 inches wide. A big box lumber store will carry this in the craft section, and will most likely even cut a board into sections for you.
- 4 carriage bolts, Size does not matter, but it has to be longer than your cheese mold, both boards, washers and nuts. If you cannot find a long enough bolt, you can use threaded rod and 4 extra nuts. Stainless works best, but it is not necessarily required.
- 4 Nuts and washers, like the bolts, stainless is more expensive but safer for food. Avoid Galvanized if possible as it will discolor over time as it contacts the cheese.
- Cheese mold
- Weights, in 1-pound increments to 20 pounds.
- Aluminum plate.

Instructions:

- Drill ½ inch holes at each corner of the boards. They need to line up with both boards, and be far enough from the edge of the board so as not to split.
- Thread carriage bolt up through both boards
- Attache nuts and washers so that ends of bolts become the "feet" of the cheese press.
- Cut a triangle out of one side of the aluminum pie plate to allow whey to drain away from cheese curd.

Use:

- To use press, fill the mold with cheesecloth wrapped cheese curds.
- Make a sandwich of bottom board, plate, mold, a can or something to press down on the cheese filled mold, and then the top board.
- Place a weight on the top board, it will press the board down as it slides down the carriage nut.
- The weight pressing down on the mold will press out liquid whey and cause it to drain out the side of the pan.

Add weights to top board as described in recipe. Too much weight makes a hard dry cheese, too little makes a crumbly overly moist cheese. The weight and time is a vital portion of the cheese recipe.

3 CHEAPER CHEESECLOTH ALTERNATIVES

I like to think I am pretty well stocked to do most things at my house. Whenever I learn to do something, or find a weakness in my plan that parts or equipment can bolster I buy several of those items, throw them in appropriately labeled boxes, on appropriately labeled shelves and then mentally check that off my list.

Neither the grocery store, nor my "local" Wal-Mart carries cheesecloth (they did carry craft cheesecloth, but it was more like a cotton minnow net, it was so course my cheese poured through it

Cheesecloth is cotton. Any un-dyed cotton should be food safe (you make your own assumption there). I would also accept nylon as a substitute.

Cheesecloth is generally 60 threads per square inch

Butter Muslin is generally 90 threads per inch, and while I am experimenting I might as well try both.

I found several things to try that worked and was inexpensive (in order of most to least expensive the following works well):

- nylon tulle mesh
- unbleached Cotton muslin
- bleached cotton

The muslin and cotton worked well with the strained yogurt. The tulle worked great for large curd cheese or straining honey.

But what worked the best was a $4.50 beer wort straining bag that I bought from the local brew store.

You need to understand what you want to accomplish and then be flexible enough mentally that you can adapt when you cannot find something that is labeled exactly how you expect.

BEST WAYS TO STORE SOFT AND HARD CHEESES

How to Store Soft and Hard Cheese to Keep It Fresh

1. **Re-Wrap the cheese**: Cheese is usually packed to have a long shelf life and to adjust to the temperatures in the supermarket or store. You will keep it in the fridge, so you need to re-wrap it according to that chilly temperature. Moreover, re-wrap the cheese carefully every time you consume it. If the cheese variety needs to be stored in paper, then change the paper on each occasion.

2. **Try cheese bags**: Cheese bags or cheese papers have pores that expose the cheese to the right amount of air they need to stay fresh. The wrap contains wax-coated paper and a thing layer of plastic, which keeps moisture from spreading. If you don't have special Cheese paper, use paper towel to wrap the cheese. Then, wrap it in a thin plastic bag or plastic paper. Make sure you fold the layers correctly and avoid the plastic touching the cheese.

3. **Place the cheese in the warmest side of your refrigerator**: If you don't have a cheese drawer, you should have one for fruit or vegetables. The recommended storage temperature is

35-45°F. The environment should also be humid. Moreover, don't place it near the meat bin, to avoid accidental freezing.

4. **Use a jar for storing cheese in the refrigerator**: Soft, semi-soft or semi-hard cheese absorbs moisture in the fridge that will cause it to lose its flavor and harden. The cheese is totally isolated to air from the fridge. In absence of a jar, you can use another airtight container. Make sure you eliminate the excessive moisture every time you consume cheese.

5. **Hard cheese needs to stay away from air**: This helps it to not dry out. You can use cheese paper, parchment or wax paper for storing this variety. However, you will need to wrap it tight or seal it with a tape, to avoid too much air. Alternatively, you can place it in a sealed class container or a sealed plastic bag. Traditionally the cheese is waxed, which we will discuss later.

6. **Protect the Cheese**: If a few days have already passed, and cheese is exposed to molding and alterations, you can protect it. Rub the slices or cut faces of the cheese with a little bit of olive oil. Then, place it in the airtight container. This way, if mold appears, it will grow on the oil, instead of the cheese. All you need to do is wipe it off.

7. **Label the Cheese**: You should label the cheese with its variety and date of purchase. You can store hard cheese for several months in the fridge. This is particularly important when you make cheese, without labeling, you never know when a cheese is ready, and without notes when you find a great recipe (or a terrible one) you won't know what caused the cheese to turn out as it did.

8. **Don't Skimp on Wrapping**: Wrapping the cheese to tight or too loose will alter its smell. By not wrapping it tight enough, you allow the cheese to dry, harden and spread its specific ammonia smell. However, when wrapping it too tight, you don't allow it to breathe. Also, never wrap it only in plastic. Plastic doesn't allow the cheese to breathe. Therefore, it's

suffocating the taste. Soon, cheese will taste like plastic and even alter faster, due to the lack of air.

9. **Remember that cheese needs to taste and smell as it did when you bought it**: If the ammonia smell is too intense, it might be time to throw it away, especially if it's a soft cheese. Also, hard cheese may harden even more or have a moist film on it. Try scraping it and see if underneath it, the cheese is still fresh.

8

HOW TO WAX HARD CHEESE

The reason you need to know how to wax hard cheese, is that the wax protects your cheese during storage. Since making cheese was the best way to store milk before refrigeration it is quite useful to know "just in case" of some manner of catastrophic disaster.

The long aging times of cheese kill any harmful bacteria that may have been present in the milk. However, anyone who has left an open block of cheese in the refrigerator knows that air will dry out your beautiful cheese into an ugly yellow rock.

The process of covering the cheese in a protective coating of wax was created to seal in moisture. Sealing with wax also protects the cheese during aging.

Over time and by experimentation I find there are simpler ways of waxing cheese, simply dipping the cheese into the wax works well, but I tend to burn my fingers, so I still like using a brush as shown in the video linked later.

Waxing Cheese By Dipping

Using this method the wax temperature is extremely hot, it is much hotter than boiling water, and wax will stick and retain heat. Work cautiously and make sure you have a good grip on the cheese before dipping. The reason you would use hot wax is because the high temperature will kill any mold that may be present on the surface fo the cheese so you won't have a problem with mold growing under your wax. However, hot wax in a danger, and dipping uses more wax than brushing.

- Heat the wax to 225-235°F, once heated turn off the stove.
- Place a piece of foil on the stove or work surface to catch any drips of wax.
- Dip the top of the cheese and let it cool.
- Then dip the bottom of the cheese and let it cool.
- Once the top and bottom surface is cool, rotate one half of the cheese edge in the wax, and let it cool. Then rotate the other half of the cheese surface and let it cool.
- Repeat the process for a second coating. If needed apply a third coating.
- When done let the wax harden. Store it in the same container used for melting with a lid on top.

9

HOW TO MAKE VEGETABLE RENNET

Most cheese was historically made with animal rennet, nowadays, a lot of cheese is made with a mold based rennet.

It is possible to make a vegetarian rennet for those that are either vegetarian, vegan, or who do not have the resources to make animal based rennet.

The biggest problem with vegetable rennet is that it becomes bitter in aged cheeses.

This means it should not be used with raw milk, or cheeses like cheddar that need aging to build their sharp taste.

List of plants used to make a vegetable rennet:

- Thistle
- Fig
- Yarrow
- Ground ivy
- Lady's Bedstraw,
- Nettle
- Pineapple

- Artichoke

Since Artichokes and Thistles are in the same family, and the easiest to find. I will use thistles gathered in a nearby field to make rennet., but as a rule of thumb if you crush and extract the sap from the greenery any of the plants above you can use it to thicken milk.

Material:

- Thistle flower head when it has turned brown, but harvest it before the plant produces the thistle down, in which case it is too late.

Or

- The Purple head of the artichoke before it makes the head

Equipment:

- Dehydrator
- Pot

Procedure:

1. Dry the flower heads and pick off the purple stamens.
2. Boil water and drop thistles into the water and let steep into a thick dark tea.
3. Strain off the liquid. This is now thistle flower rennet.
4. The rennet can now be added to warmed milk to curdle it and begin the cheese making process.

Note:

Most cheese recipes using commercial rennet are in the teaspoon/tablespoon amounts, I started using a traditional recipe amount, but ended up using ½ cup of my homemade rennet to get a good result.

HOW TO MAKE YOGURT

Yogurt uses a thermophilic starter, that means "heart loving". The great thing about cultures is, that if you store them correctly, you only have to buy one once.

For this recipe you will need a yogurt with a live and active culture. Commonly this is sold as a healthy choice to help with "gut" issues.

Ingredients

- Fresh Milk
- Fresh yogurt (either homemade or store bought labeled "live and active culture").

Procedure

1. Heat 2 cups of milk to 185°F) on the range top or in a microwave. (Be careful not heat too high)
2. cool to room temperature.(at least 112-115°F)
3. Add one heaping tablespoon of yogurt to get the live culture.
4. Mix the yogurt into the milk thoroughly with a fork or a whisk.

5. Keep the mixture at (110ºF) for 8-10 hours until a firm yogurt
   has set. (a sterile mason jar placed in a warm water bath inside
   a crock pot on low works well. Monitor the temperature
6. Cool the yogurt in the refrigerator for a couple of hours. As
   the yogurt cools it will thicken.

Tips and Advice:

You can use almost any kind of milk (except box ultra high pasteurized). I have even used goat milk. Of course the more fat the richer and thicker the final yogurt will be.

Homemade yogurt is not as sweet as store bought yogurt because it does not have sugar added. You could add sweetener (a tablespoon or so) when you add the yogurt to the warm milk, but I like adding vanilla.

If you want to add fruit do so after the incubation period of step 5, otherwise you risk messing up the bacteria by adding the bacteria from the fruit.

This lasts in the fridge for about 10 days because it does not have the preservatives of store bought packaged product.

11

THERMOPHILIC CHEESE STARTER

Heat Loving Cultures are used to make cheeses that can be heated to 130 degrees, this means yogurt and many Italian cheeses like parmesan, provolone, mozzarella and Swiss, and Monterey jack

Since there are varieties of cultures (like yeasts) and we are starting with yogurt, the finished flavor may be slightly different from store bought cheese cultures.

This process begins with the yogurt from the previous chapter:

1. Pour your homemade yogurt into a full size sterile ice cube tray and put into your freezer.
2. Once frozen, remove the cubes and put into a clean sealed container or plastic freezer bags. Label to distinguish it from your Mesophilic culture.
3. The cubes are each 1 ounce of thermophilic starter..
4. Add these cubes (thawed) to your recipes as required. The cubes will keep for about one month.

12

GREEK YOGURT

Greek Yogurt I learned how versatile it is, as well as how healthy.

Because it is concentrated yogurt, it contains nearly double the protein as the same amount of yogurt. Its thickness makes it feel rich but it is low fat and low sugar. If you use it plain it can replace sour cream in all sorts of recipes. It turns tomato soup into a rich tomato cream sauce. You can use it to make smoothies, as a dip with burritos, as a cheese on quesadillas. It lends itself to all sorts of creative cooking. However, I love it in Tzatziki cucumber sauce.

As a side benefit, because you can make it yourself from homemade yogurt, Greek Yogurt is sustainable. Also, because it is a way to extend the shelf life of milk, it is great for homesteaders and preppers. (It's also significantly cheaper to turn yogurt to Greek yogurt than to just buy it ready-made.)

I learned how to do this before I learned to make yogurt, so you can either use store bought yogurt or hold on two weeks for the yogurt recipe…

Ingredients

- Yogurt
- Equipment
- Cheesecloth
- Bowl
- String

Procedure

- Line bowl with four layers of cheesecloth
- Dump Yogurt into bowl
- Bring corners of cloth together to make a "bag" or yogurt. Tie together with string
- Lift bag out of bowl and hang above bowl.
- Let drain 8 – 10 hours until whey has drained out of yogurt causing it to thicken

You can use the whey for other things. Most notably, it is used in baking homemade bread. I have also heard of people using whey for lacto-fermentation of vegetables, but I have to clear off some other things from the list before I can try that.

Spoon it into a container and refrigerate for up to six days.

I find this yogurt to be pretty mild and pleasing, it is like eating cream cheese. You can add flavorings, but don't go overboard it only takes a little to overpower the yogurt.

I have tried strawberry jelly, but so far my favorite has been some honey and crushed pecans.

Granola mixed with this yogurt is a healthy and satisfying snack as well.

13

HOMEMADE TZATZKI SAUCE

Gyros with Tzatziki sauce is as good to me as a grilled burger. I have tried several times to get this recipe right (by experimentation and guesswork) but once I started looking online I found out simple it really is to make homemade Tzatziki Sauce.

There are as many ways to make this as there are cooks who make it. It is made thick and eaten like a salad, made thin and drunk like a smoothie, or like the recipe here, made medium thick and used as a condiment.

The only common denominator in most Tzatziki recipes is the use of cucumber and yogurt. However, traditional Greek recipes call for dill as well. Oils, spices and nuts are often added in regional recipes.

Ingredients

- 1 Medium cucumber
- Salt
- 2 cups Greek Yogurt
- 2 tablespoon chopped fresh mint (optional)
- 4 teaspoons chopped fresh dill (optional)

- 2 teaspoons fresh lemon juice (optional)
- 4 garlic cloves, minced (optional)

Preparation

- Peel and slice cucumber in half
- With a sharp pointed spoon, scrape out seeds
- Slice cucumber and place cucumber in colander; sprinkle with 1/4 teaspoon salt to draw out moisture.
- Let stand 30 minutes.
- Combine cucumber, yogurt, and any optional ingredients desired in a blender or food processor
- Process until well blended. (see all the water released from pureeing the cucumber. If you did not use salt on cucumber slices then this mixture would be like a soup.
- Refrigerate at least 1 hour before serving.

14

HOW TO MAKE CREME FRAICHE

Crème Fraîche is a fermented dairy product used in both hot and cold French cuisine, while now it is seen as a "gourmet" Food, it was traditionally used as a economic "peasant food".

As a practical person, I am a big fan of what is called "peasant food", local, nutritious, inexpensive, and plentiful food that is used by the lower economic class as staples.

I figure if it was used to keep the average peasant alive in the 1600s it would work to keep me alive if I had to deal with the End of The World As We Know it...

Now back to French cuisine...

Crème fraîche is a thick fermented liquid cream, like yogurt. Because it has greater than 30% fat content It can be used to finish hot sauces without curdling.

Making it is pretty simple. All you do is add a starter culture to heavy cream, and allowing it to stand at appropriate temperature until thick.

What starter culture should you use?

Buttermilk works well.

The ratio of cream to buttermilk doesn't really matter all that much.

Add more buttermilk and you'll need less time for it to thicken (but it will be less creamy).

Add more, and it takes longer to thicken, but tastes better.

One tablespoon per cup (that's a 1:16 ratio) is the closest to the European product.

With a 1:16 ratio It will be very rich and creamy about 12-hours after mixing.

You can also halt the process early by just refrigerating it to stop the bacterial action.

This is useful if you want a thinner Mexican-style Crema Agria for drizzling over tacos or nachos.

Yes, I am talking about room temperature milk, but for the safety nellies, the good bacteria from the buttermilk prevents the dangerous bacteria from taking over.

Store in the refrigerator for up to 2 weeks.

15

HOW TO MAKE CREAM CHEESE

This is a very simple recipe, no measuring or special equipment needed. This is a great project for someone that wants to introduce a kid to cheese making.

Room temperature does impact the inoculation time, if your home is 72°F or higher this cheese will take a lot less time to make. Do not get discouraged if your home is cooler and it looks like nothing is happening. The culture does not work fast when it is cold....

Ingredients

- 1 quart light cream or half and half (A package of commercial culture can inoculate up to two gallons of milk)
- 1 package Mesophilic culture

Procedure

- Allow your half and half to reach room temperature, your cheese will set more quickly if it isn't refrigerator chilled when you add the starter culture. For the video, I kept sitting it out, and the wife kept putting it back in the fridge. I would have been mad, but she thought I left it out accidentally as was trying to be helpful. The lesson is COMMUNICATE….)

- Pour milk into a container, I see many using flat baking dishes, but I used a bowl in the video listed later because I did not have enough plastic wrap to cover a flat dish. Technically it makes no difference as long as it is nonreactive.
- Add your culture to the milk, sprinkling it over the top.
- Let the culture set for a couple minutes before stirring. Mix very well.
- Cover and let set from 8 to 12 hours.
- When the cream cheese is set, it will have the texture of yogurt. (It may appear to you nothing is happening, but here is where you wait and be patient. When I made it in the video, I started at 6pm and at 7am the next morning the milk was not coagulating very much at all.)
- Once it looks like yogurt. Drain the whey out by dumping the milk into a square of butter-muslin sitting in a large pot. I then collect the corners and tie into a bag. Then tie a string to the bag and let drain over the pot for 12 hours.
- Once the whey has drained, package and store in the fridge. If you want to stir in herbs, fruit, jam, or honey go for it. Be careful, it doesn't to take as much flavor as you would expect so don't go overboard.

This does not store for as long as commercial cream cheese. It is also not as mild. On the plus side it has no preservatives or chemicals.

16

HOW TO MAKE CLARIFIED BUTTER
AKA GHEE

This really ought not to be called ghee as true ghee in India is made more with yogurt than butter, but here in America the distinction between ghee and clarified butter is not as strongly enforced.

My wife likes ghee because she can use it on her whole 30 diet, I like it because it has a smoke point of 482°F.

I will share the method to make Ghee that I most often use. I tend to make this often as it is a preferred oil in my wife's 21 day fix eating plan.

How to Make Clarified Butter

Ingredients:

- One Pound of UNSALTED butter

Procedure:

- Place butter in medium saucepan over medium-high heat.
- Bring butter to boil. This takes approximately 2 to 3 minutes.

- Once boiling, reduce the heat to medium.
- The butter will form a foam which will disappear.
- Ghee is done when a second foam forms on top of butter, and the butter turns golden. This takes approximately 7 to 8 minutes.
- Brown milk solids will be in bottom of pan.
- Gently pour into heatproof container through fine mesh strainer or cheesecloth.
- Store in airtight container being sure to keep free from moisture.

Ghee does not need refrigeration and will keep in airtight container for up to 1 month.

MAKE BUTTER WITH POWDERED MILK

In a grid down scenario, if you don't have cows or milk goats you may think you will have to give up things like butter. However, if you have stored dry milk you could just make your own butter from powdered milk

In my experience, making butter from powdered milk is very easy and it only takes a couple of minutes. Plus, the taste and the texture is close if not identical.

The only difference I have seen is that this butter does not melt when used in cooking recipes. I tried to make an Alfredo and the butter browned and crumbled. (however I did find that to be tasty it just was unexpected).

I have used this recipe in several talks about DIY prepping, and it is a great recipe to try with kids. If you use a mason jar blender it i even easier plus it comes ready to store.

Keep your powdered milk butter in a sealed container in the fridge and use in a month or so as typical dried milk is close to becoming rancid by the time you buy it.

How to Make Butter with Powdered Milk

Ingredients

- 3/4 cup powdered milk
- 1/3 cup water
- 1/4 cup oil

Optional

- yellow food coloring
- salt
- butter flavoring

Procedure

- Add the powdered milk to a bowl (easier with a blender or food processor).
- Add the water and then the oil.
- Mix rapidly until it starts to thicken. Keep mixing until it starts getting thick.
- You can then add in butter flavoring, yellow food coloring and salt at this point if desired.

This recipe will make about 3/4 cup of "butter"

MAKING SOFT CURD CHEESE FROM POWDERED MILK

As with most foods, fat makes cheese taste better, so if you have whole milk powder your cheese will have a richer taste. Unfortunately, almost all milk stored long term is the non-fat kind as the milk fats cause the powdered milk to go rancid very quickly. As a matter of fact, dry milk from your grocery is either already rancid, or very close to its 6 month shelf life. This is one item that I recommend buying from specialty disaster prep stores. This way the product was packaged in #10 cans immediately after manufacture so it has a much better shelf life.

Equipment:

- Large stainless steel stock pot
- Long handled stainless steel spoon
- Cheesecloth
- Colander

Ingredients:

- 3 cups powdered milk
- 6 cups water

- Vinegar

Instructions:

1. Reconstitute your dried milk, either follow the directions on the milk package or combine 3 cups of powdered milk with 6 cups of cold water in a large stock pot.
2. Stir until the milk is totally dissolved in the water.
3. Heat the milk over medium low heat until it reaches 120°F.
4. You need a good cooking thermometer to make cheese, but if you don't have one yet heat the milk until it is hot to the touch, but not scalding
5. Turn off the heat and add 1/4 cup of vinegar to the milk.
6. Stir and let the milk sit for 10 minutes.
7. You should see the curds separate from the whey, if not add an additional 1/4 cup of vinegar and wait another 10 minutes.
8. (There are also some neat recipes online for making a very primitive plastic using a very similar method. I find it to be a neat science demonstration for kids, but I find it to be too brittle for any real use)
9. Place a sheet of cheesecloth in a colander. Pour the curds into the cheesecloth. If desired, set the colander over a large bowl and collect the whey.
10. Whey is useful for replacing water in many recipes like:
11. Baking
12. Soups
13. Soaking grains
14. Smoothies and shakes
15. Watering your garden
16. I find that the dog really likes it (it has a lot of proteins)
17. Rinse the cheese curds under cold running water and let drain.
18. Transfer to a covered container and store in the refrigerator.

19

MAKING MOCK PARMESAN CHEESE
FROM DEHYDRATED MILK

I know it sounds silly, but if I ever have to resort to living solely off my food stores alone I am afraid of food fatigue. That's why I try to only store the foods I like to eat, but no matter how much I store now, or how much I try to store good tasting foods, the local BBQ pit is only a short drive away.

To combat appetite fatigue I try to find multiple ways to cook the same items to get different tastes (and textures). That is one reason I whole heartedly endorse.

Peggy Layton and Vicki Tate's "Cooking with Home Storage" book series. Those ladies show how to make hundreds of food recipes using the same simple ingredients.

Her ingenuity, imagination and skill can help you achieve amazing results with your home storage if you put in the time to practice and learn for yourself which recipes you and your family likes BEFORE you don't have any other options.

This recipe for mock Parmesan Cheese from Dehydrated Milk uses the soft curd cheese described in the previous chapter.

How to make Mock Parmesan Cheese from Dehydrated Milk

Equipment:

- Bowl
- Fork
- Cookie Sheet

Ingredients:

- Dehydrated Milk "Ricotta" Cheese
- Cheese salt to taste

Instructions:

1. Place curds into a bowl and stir with a fork to break up into small pieces.
2. Spread cheese on a cookie sheet and dry for about 10 minutes in a 150ºF oven. Alternatively you can use a dehydrator.
3. Salt to taste

This can be used in place of Parmesan or mixed with 1/4 to 1/3 commercially dried Parmesan cheese.

Store in a refrigerator or freezer A pleasant flavor change takes place after about 3 months of aging under refrigeration.

HOW TO MAKE TOFU

Basically tofu is a bean curd made by coagulating soy milk and then pressing the resulting curds into soft white blocks. It's very similar to making a vinegar based cheese like ricotta.

To do make tofu you only need soymilk, a coagulant, a pot, spoon, sieve, and a way to press out the water. I used my cheese mold, but you could use a saucer pressing down on the curds in your sieve.

There are three basic types of coagulants; Salts, Acids, and Enzymes. Enzyme tofu production is beyond my scope as a home chemist so I won't discuss them. I have also read that a lot of the medical problems some attribute to tofu stems from the use of enzymes but I am not a doctor, so you should research that yourself.

Salt coagulants

- **Calcium sulfate** (gypsum): The traditional and most widely used coagulant to produce Chinese-style tofu. It produces a tofu that is tender but slightly brittle in texture. The coagulant itself has no perceivable taste. Use of this coagulant also makes a tofu that is rich in calcium.

- **Magnesium chloride** (Nigari) salts or calcium chloride (Lushui): These are the coagulants used to make tofu with a smooth and tender texture. In Japan, a white powder called *nigari*, which consists primarily of magnesium chloride, is produced from seawater after the sodium chloride is removed and the water evaporated.
- **Magnesium Sulfate** (Epsom salt), is readily available and cheap, so for the beginner or first time user, this is a great coagulant to use

Acid coagulants

Can affect the taste of the tofu more than salts, and vary in efficacy and texture. But the two most used are

- Vinegar (acetic acid)
- Lemon Juice (citric acid)

The recipe I used called for acid and it said either distilled while vinegar or lemon juice could be used interchangeably. I used lemon juice.

How to Make tofu:

Ingredients:

- 1/2 gallon of Soymilk
- Hot Water
- 1/2 cup Vinegar

Procedure:

- Boil your soymilk. Stir frequently, this scorches easily.

- Once it is boiling simmer for 7 minutes. (Stir frequently)
- Mix 1 ½ cup of hot water with ½ cup of acid.
- Once the milk has simmered remove from heat and stir in 1/3 of your acid into the milk. Stir very thoroughly.
- Keep the spoon in the pot and stop stirring. This sets up eddies in the milk to ensure a good mixing. When the milk stops moving, remove the spoon and sprinkle the second third of the acid on the top of the milk.
- Cover the pot and let sit for 20 minutes.
- Check the milk, the milk should curdle and the liquid should be clear but yellowish. If the milk has not fully separated add the last third of the acid, stir, cover and let sit another 3 minutes or so. You will most likely need all the acid. The more acid you use the more you will taste it. By adding it in steps you may reduce the amount you will need to use.
- Ladle the curds into a sieve lined with cheesecloth.
- Lift the edges of the cheesecloth and lift the bundle out of the sieve and let place it into your press.
- The weights and press times will change depending on how firm you want your tofu. 10 minutes with a quart mason jar of water will give softer tofu, double the weight and time for a firmer tofu. I used a quart jar of honey and 20 minutes and it turned out pretty good.
- Once it has been pressed place the tofu in a bowl of cold water for everything to set.

Tofu tastes best a few hours after it's been made.

If you make your tofu in the morning, it will be at its peak at dinner..

If you will store the tofu for more than a day, cover the tofu with water. Since it is preservative free, home-made tofu should not be kept more than a couple of days –

If you intend to eat the tofu on the same day don't put any water in the container. Put on an airtight lid, and store in the refrigerator until ready to eat.

Alternatively you can freeze your tofu. If you do that, the water crystals will form holes in your tofu changing its texture to a more meat similar texture.

21

HOW TO MAKE HOMEMADE TVP

When I first got into the prepping lifestyle the first thing I bought was a big can of TVP. I figured it was cheap. Since it had a 30 year shelf life so I could not go wrong…

I went WRONG…. Years later I actually opened the can and tried it. I hated it, and I did not know what to so with it.

Fast Forward a few years. I learned how to make tofu. From that, I had the idea to see if I could make TVP

What is TVP?

Basically Textured Vegetable Protein (TVP) is a meat replacement or meat extender made from defatted soy flour. This is what is left after you squeeze out soybean oil. TVP is also known as textured soy protein (TSP), soy meat, or soya meat

Its popular in food storage because it is cheap, quick to cook, contains no fat. Additionally, it has a protein content equal to that of real meat.

Making TVP is an industrial process where hot soy flour is extruded into various shapes (chunks, flakes, nuggets, grains, and strips) and sizes. The defatted thermoplastic proteins are heated to 150-200°C, which breaks them into a fibrous, insoluble, porous mass that can soak up as much as three times its weight in liquids.

How TVP is Used

TVP can be mixed with ground meat to a ratio of up to 1:3 (rehydrated TVP to meat) without reducing the quality of the final product.

TVP is primarily used as a meat substitute due to its very low cost at less than a third the price of ground beef, and when cooked together will help retain more weight from the meat by absorbing juices normally lost.

Now, this process is beyond my scope, but in doing research caused by my picking up that bean book I figured if I can make tofu I surely can make TVP, so I searched until I found a recipe that gave me a workaround to make a product that is very similar in usage to real TVP.

A Homemade Workaround to DIY TVP

Basically I froze my homemade tofu for 48 hours to give it that meat like texture I discussed earlier. I then let it thaw and once that was done, I simply crumbled it up and dehydrated it.

The tofu dried very quickly and resembled the prepper food "hamburger rocks". The only difference was that the TVP was lighter in color, and did not have a taste.

However, no taste is a good thing, as the pores created in the freezing process will suck up the cooking water and make the TVP take on the flavor of whatever you a cooking it with.

I like this best in homemade chili.

HOW TO MAKE SEITAN: VEGETARIAN WHEAT MEAT

My search to find alternative food sources has led me to learn how to make Seitan. Seitan is basically the protein portion of wheat that has been flavored to mimic the taste of meat. You might not be familiar with the name, but if you have ever had mock chicken, beef, or pork at a Chinese restaurant. You have had seitan.

Making it is pretty easy, but to the uninitiated it looks a little gross. In its cooked, but not finished form, my wife wanted to throw it away… Cut up and put in chili, she doesn't know she is not eating chicken…

Making it is simple, you basically make a dough out of flour and water. Once the dough is made you rinse out the starch leaving a stringy mass of wheat gluten. You then flavor by simmering in broth and BAM – you have a passable meat substitute.

Ingredients:

- 5 lb. bag of flour, any flour will work, but the more gluten the more seitan you will get
- Lots of water

- Flavorings: I used chicken broth, garlic and herb powder, soy sauce, dales meat marinade, and a large onion.

Tools:

- Large bowl
- Colander
- Crockpot

Procedure:

- Dump the flour in the bowl and add water to make a dough. Add water in a little at a time because you do not want to make a paste.
- Once it is kneaded into a single solid ball, cover with water and let soak for 20 minutes or so. The water should be a little milky.
- Next, knead the dough a little under the water, the water should get very milky. That's the starch separating out …
- Drain into a colander and start running water over it. The water should be lukewarm and not under a lot of pressure. You want to gently rinse the start away rather than blast it apart. Knead the dough under the water and watch the dough change consistency.
- The dough will become stringy and stretchy, and I thought it looked a lot like brains… But this is how you want it to look.
- Keep kneading until the water runs clear and its one solid mass.
- At this point you need to cook your gluten. Flavorings are up to you, you can use stock or Italian seasonings, or even sausage seasonings. I saw a cool recipe for seitan pepperoni that I am going to try one day.
- Some boil the seitan until it floats, but for ease I used a slow cooker. I simply dumped in a jar of canned stock, and one onion, along with whatever cool seasonings I had in the

cabinet. I cooked on high for about 2 hours and then left it on low for the rest of the night

Its not brain science or rocket surgery, its just a little messy kneading all that dough, but hey, if I can do it, you can too…

After a couple days in the fridge, I sliced a ½ slab from the ball and fried it with barbeque sauce, I then broke it into chicken nugget sized chunks and stabbed them with a metal skewer and left them where the wife would find them… She thought it was pork BBQ and said it was really good (she did gag a little when I told her it was the wheat brain I made the weekend before)…. It tasted like a McRib from McDonalds (which it was probably pretty close to it).

I cubed the rest and dehydrated for chili later. This stuff has no taste to speak of, but it does have a "meaty" texture. Its kinda cool in a weird sort of way

PLEASE REVIEW

Please visit my Amazon Author Page at:

https://amazon.com/author/davidnash

if you like my work, you can really help me by publishing a review on Amazon.

The link to review this work at Amazon is:

https://www.amazon.com/review/create-review?asin=B07YGLJKSD

LINKS TO VIDEOS

The Basics of Making Homemade Cheese: Playlist

http://yt.vu/p/PLZH3jGjLQ0rDLbkuMOPKEe_L0juG_oG_X

How to Make Fresh Mozzarella Cheese at Home

https://youtu.be/GhjuJ1fIMUg

How to Make Farmhouse Cheddar I: Equipment, Ingredients, and Using Rennet

https://youtu.be/91COo5YjGho

How to Make Farmhouse Cheddar II: Cutting and Draining the Curd

https://youtu.be/udmLX7eh22w

How to Make Farmhouse Cheddar III: Molding and Pressing the Curd

https://youtu.be/YA2lCIGFgJk

How to Make an Inexpensive Cheese Press

https://youtu.be/qdj2MQVuMhs

Can't Find Cheesecloth? 3 Cheaper Cheesecloth Alternatives

https://youtu.be/w7wfW6eebCg

How to Wax Hard Cheese

https://youtu.be/Z5GJ1H63UjU

How to Make a Mesophilic Cheese Culture

https://youtu.be/Vyj3hYiq2vg

How to Make Greek Yogurt

https://youtu.be/xu85uVv_isY

How to Make Tzatzki Sauce

https://youtu.be/DDz_LzknKtw

How to Make Cream Cheese

https://youtu.be/UZawP-JL2m8

How to Make Clarified Butter aka Ghee

https://www.youtube.com/watch?v=0iVvrGAubAU

How to Make Butter with Powdered Milk

https://youtu.be/v0F2CgDqM6w

How to Make Soft Curd Cheese from Powdered Milk

https://youtu.be/YHTonIBbr08

How to Make Mock Parmesan Cheese from Dehydrated Milk

https://youtu.be/9H6knuYeL2Y

How to Make Tofu

https://youtu.be/GsX6dvAXfoM

How to Make TVP

https://youtu.be/pS3D1PADiBo

How to Make Seitan

https://youtu.be/fg8maVmAS60

The Basics of Making
Homemade Wine
and Vinegar
Homestead Basics Book 5
David Nash

Why Make Homemade Wine

There are many reasons to make homemade wine, from health to being cost conscious, but for me it's the experience of doing something on my own and freeing myself from reliance on a store for something I enjoy.

This freedom soon translates into artistic license. Once you learn the technique and science behind wine making you are free to experiment. Then you can create wines from fruits and vegetables that you grow.

Making wine can become a hobby, or just a way to put food aside. Therefore, you can spend as much or as little time, effort, and resources as you desire. I personally enjoy a cold glass of sweet tea much more than a glass of chardonnay. However, I DO enjoy seeing others enjoy the products of my labor and skill. It is pleasing to me, and worth the effort to give a bottle of MY wine as a gift, or to enjoy it with someone.

Homemade Wine is Healthy

We all know about the French paradox. The French as a culture eat as much (or more) of the fatty foods as we do but have a much lower instance of heart disease than out American culture. While the entire reason for this is unclear. There is much evidence that the flavonoids found in the skins, seeds, stems, and pulp of dark grapes protect against heart attacks, blood clots, hardening of the arteries, Alzheimer's, and kidney stones. It has also been bound that fermenting grape juice allows more of the flavonoids to be released than pressing into juice alone.

Making Wine is a Good Disaster Prep

From a disaster prep standpoint, making wine has two good purposes. Utility of them can be decided upon by the reader. The first is barter. If you put aside a bottle or two from every batch of wine you make, over the course of a year you will have a decent store of wine, This collection could be traded for items you may not have. The second is that throughout history fermented beverages were served almost exclusively in place of water. This is because without modern infrastructure, it can become difficult to purify water. The fermentation process kills many harmful organisms. Additionally, the alcohol contained in wine serves as a good preservative.

If you like this Introduction to The Basics of Making Homemade Wine and Vinegar, you can find it on Amazon.

ALSO BY DAVID NASH

Fiction

The Deserter: Legion Chronicles Book 1

The Revolution: Legion Chronicles Book 2

The Return: Legion Chronicles Book 3

The Warrior: Legion Chronicles Book 4

Homestead Basics

The Basics of Raising Backyard Chickens

The Basics of Raising Backyard Rabbits

The Basics of Beginning Beekeeping

The Basics of Making Homemade Cheese

The Basics of Making Homemade Wine and Vinegar

The Basics of Making Homemade Cleaning Supplies

The Basics of Baking

The Basics of Food Preservation

The Basics of Food Storage

The Basics of Cooking Meat

The Basics of Make Ahead Mixes

The Basics of Beginning Leatherwork

Non Fiction

21 Days to Basic Preparedness

52 Prepper Projects

52 Prepper Projects for Parents and Kids

52 Unique Techniques for Stocking Food for Preppers

Basic Survival: A Beginner's Guide

Building a Get Home Bag

Handguns for Self Defense

How I Built a Ferrocement "Boulder Bunker"

New Instructor Survival Guide

The Prepper's Guide to Foraging

The Prepper's Guide to Foraging: Revised 2nd Edition

The Ultimate Guide to Pepper Spray

Understanding the Use of Handguns for Self Defense

Note and Record Books

Correction Officer's Notebook

Get Healthy Notebook

Rabbitry Records

Collections and Box Sets

Preparedness Collection

Legion Chronicles Trilogy

Translations

La Guía Definitiva Para El Spray De Pimienta

Multimedia

Alternative Energy

Firearm Manuals

Military Manuals 2 Disk Set

ABOUT THE AUTHOR

 David Nash is a suburban homesteader with chickens, bees, rabbits, and a couple of goats in his suburban yard. For a while he even had an extensive aquaponics setup in his basement, until his long-suffering wife made him eat all the fish.

He knows how to raise animals humanely, simply, and without angering the neighbors. Dave runs a popular YouTube channel on DIY homesteading as well as being the author of several books on DIY preparedness and urban homesteading topics.

In fact, the tips shown in this book contributed to him receiving the third highest preparedness score on the TV show Doomsday Preppers

He is a father and a husband. He enjoys time with his young son William Tell and his school teacher wife Genny. When not working, writing, creating content for YouTube, playing on his self-reliance blog, or smoking award-winning BBQ he is asleep.

amazon.com/author/davidnash

facebook.com/booksbynash

youtube.com//tngun

goodreads.com/david_allen_nash

twitter.com/dnash1974

instagram.com/shepherdschool

pinterest.com/tngun